The 5-step Writing Master plan
Craft Compelling Stories and Transform Your Writing Skills

The 5-step Writing Master plan

Craft Compelling Stories and Transform Your Writing Skills

Published by Word Tangles, Tripura Road Khanapara (Guwahati)

2023, FirstEdition

ISBN 979-8-388540-20-1

Edited by: *Meghamallicka Dutta*
Cover design: *Vihaan Baruah*
Typesetting by: *Clemens Lode*

Printed on acid-free, unbleached paper.

Subscribe to our newsletter at https://wordtangles.com. Or write to biswajit@wordtangles.com.

Dedication

To my dearest Dad,

Thank you for instilling in me a love for language and literature from a young age. Your passion for words and storytelling has inspired me to pursue my own writing journey. Your guidance and support have been invaluable in shaping me into the writer I am today. This book is dedicated to you, with gratitude and love.

And to all the aspiring writers out there,

May this book be a source of inspiration and guidance as you embark on your own writing journey. Whether you dream of writing a novel, a memoir, or a blog, may these 5 steps help you craft compelling stories and transform your writing skills. This book is dedicated to you, with the hope that it will empower you to unleash your creativity and share your unique voice with the world.

Sincerely,
Biswajit D Baruah

Introduction

Writing is both an art and a craft. It requires creativity, imagination, and a deep understanding of language, but it also demands discipline, practice, and a willingness to revise and refine one's work. Whether you are a seasoned writer looking to hone your skills or a beginner hoping to embark on your writing journey, this book offers a 5-step master plan to help you craft compelling stories and transform your writing skills. From developing a clear idea and structure to refining your style and editing your work, these steps provide a road map to guide you through the writing process and unlock your full potential as a writer. Whether your goal is to write a novel, a memoir, or a screenplay, or simply an article this book will help you bring your stories to life and share them with the world.

There is no greater agony than bearing an untold story inside you.

—Maya Angelou

Writing is easy. All you have to do is cross out the wrong words.

—Mark Twain

Contents

Foreword

> Writing is an act of courage. It requires an immense amount of vulnerability and a willingness to put yourself out there, to be seen and heard. But it also offers the potential for great reward, for the satisfaction of sharing your unique perspective and connecting with others through your words.

—Brené Brown

As an avid reader and aspiring writer, I have always been fascinated by the art of storytelling. There is something magical about the way a well-crafted story can transport us to different worlds, inspire us, and connect us with others. But as much as I love reading, I have often felt intimidated by the idea of writing my own stories. Where do I start? How do I know if my writing is any good? These are questions that have often held me back from pursuing my writing dreams.

That's why I was thrilled to discover this book. The 5-step writing master plan is a practical guide for anyone who wants to improve their writing skills and tell better stories. What I appreciate about this book is the way it breaks down the writing process into manageable steps, from developing a clear idea to revising and editing your work. Each step is presented in a clear and concise way.

But what really sets this book apart is the way it balances creativity and technique. Whether you're struggling with finding the right words or figuring out how to structure your story, this book has you covered.

As a reader, I can confidently say that this book will help you become a better writer.

Ashish Shukla

Preface

Writing has always been a passion of mine. From an early age, I was drawn to the power of storytelling and the way that words can transport us to different worlds, evoke emotions, and connect us with others. But as much as I loved writing, I often struggled with the process. It felt overwhelming and intimidating, and I didn't know where to start or how to improve.

Over time, however, I began to realize that writing was not just a matter of talent or inspiration, but also of discipline and practice. I started to read books on writing, attend workshops and classes, and experiment with different techniques and styles. As I continued to write and learn, I developed a 5-step master plan that helped me break down the writing process into manageable steps and unlock my full potential as a writer.

That's why I wrote this book. I wanted to share the lessons I've learned and the techniques I've developed with other aspiring writers. I know firsthand how daunting the writing process can be, and I wanted to create a resource that would help writers of all levels overcome their fears, unleash their creativity, and craft compelling stories.

This book is the result of years of writing, reading, learning, and refining. It's a product of my own journey as a writer, and I hope that it will inspire and empower others to embark on their own writing journeys.

I am honored to share this book with you and hope that it will help you achieve your writing goals and tell the stories that only you can tell.

Biswajit D Baruah Muscat, Oman, March 31, 2023

The Art of Planning your Writing

When writing, planning is often overlooked, as many aspiring writers focus primarily on their creative flair and storytelling abilities. However, it is an essential skill that a writer must develop in order to craft compelling stories that captivate readers from the very beginning. Mastering the planning process not only helps one structure the narrative effectively, but it also provides one with a roadmap that guides through the various stages of writing. This makes the process more efficient and enjoyable. In this chapter, we will discuss why planning is crucial, as it lays the foundation for a well-organized and coherent story. We will explore the different approaches to planning, from meticulous outlining to more flexible methods that leave room for spontaneity and discovery. Finally, we will provide practical tips and strategies for creating an effective writing plan, tailored to your individual needs and goals as a writer. By understanding the importance of planning and implementing the techniques discussed in this chapter, you will be well-equipped to transform your writing skills and craft stories that resonate with your audience.

Why Planning Matters

It is crucial to understand that without a proper plan, even the most creative ideas can fall apart. Planning your writing enables you to create a compelling narrative that draws readers in and keeps them engaged throughout the story. By dedicating time and effort to plan your writing, you ensure that you have a clear roadmap to follow, which helps you avoid unnecessary detours.

Planning is a powerful tool that enables you to:

Organize your thoughts and ideas: Planning helps you arrange your ideas in a logical order, ensuring that your story flows smoothly and makes sense to your readers. This organization process also allows you to prioritize the most important aspects of your narrative, ensuring that you focus on what truly matters.

Create a cohesive and logical structure : A well-planned story has a strong structure that guides readers through the narrative, making it easier for them to understand and follow the plot. A solid structure also contributes to the overall pacing of your story, maintaining readers' interest and preventing them from getting lost or bored.

Identify gaps in your knowledge or understanding: During the planning process, you may discover areas where you need to conduct further research or clarify your thoughts. Identifying these gaps early on allows you to address them before you begin writing, leading to a more polished and well-informed final product.

Save time by reducing the need for extensive rewrites: A thorough plan can help you avoid major plot holes, inconsistencies, and other issues that may require time-consuming rewrites later in the writing process. By investing in planning upfront, you can save valuable time and effort, allowing you to focus on refining your prose and perfecting your storytelling.

In summary, planning plays a vital role in the writing process, setting the stage for compelling and well-structured stories. By mastering the art of planning, you can transform your writing skills and create narratives that resonate with your readers.

Approaches to Planning

It is crucial to understand that planning is not a one-size-fits-all process. Each writer has their unique thought process, preferences, and creative style, which can significantly impact their approach to planning. We will explore a variety of planning methods, allowing you to choose and adapt the techniques that best suit your individual needs and writing style. By understanding the diverse approaches to planning, you will be better equipped to develop a tailored planning process that empowers you to craft compelling stories and enhance your writing skills.

Outlining

Outlining is a fundamental technique that can significantly improve the overall organization and structure of your work. This methodical approach provides a clear roadmap for your writing, helping you to navigate the complexities of your narrative or article with ease.

Outlining is the process of creating a detailed list or framework for your writing. This approach involves breaking your work down into sections, chapters, or even individual scenes, and then noting the key points, events, and character developments that occur within each. By mapping out the trajectory of your story or article in advance, you can ensure that your work maintains a consistent and coherent flow, allowing readers to follow the narrative with ease.

To create an effective outline, follow these steps:

Step 1: Determine the beginning, middle, and end of your story or article Before diving into the specifics, take a step back and consider the broader arc of your narrative or article. Identify the critical turning points and milestones that will shape your work, such as the inciting incident, climax, and resolution.

Step 2: Break down each section into smaller, manageable parts Once you have a general sense of your work's overall structure, start dissecting each section into more detailed components. This might involve dividing a novel into chapters, a screenplay into acts and scenes, or an article into subheadings and paragraphs.

Step 3: List the main events, ideas, or topics for each part With your work broken down into smaller units, focus on identifying the essential elements within each segment. This could include crucial plot developments, character arcs, thematic explorations, or key arguments and supporting evidence in the case of non-fiction writing.

Step 4: Order these events or ideas in a logical and coherent manner Finally, arrange the components of your outline in a manner that reflects the natural progression of your story or argument. This step will help you establish a clear narrative or logical flow that guides readers through your work, ensuring that they remain engaged and invested in the story or topic at hand.

By creating a detailed outline, you can gain a more comprehensive understanding of your work's structure and scope, allowing you to approach the writing process with a sense of clarity and direction. As you progress through your outline, you may find that some elements need to be adjusted or reworked, and that's perfectly fine. Outlines are meant to serve as a flexible guide that can be adapted as needed to best serve your story or article. Embracing the outlining process can ultimately help you craft more compelling and well-organized stories, propelling you towards greater success in your writing endeavours.

Mind Mapping

Another valuable technique to consider is mind mapping. This creative and visual approach enables you to brainstorm, organize, and explore the relationships between different ideas, themes, or concepts within your writing project. Mind mapping encourages creativity, allowing you to uncover new connections or insights that can enhance your work's depth and complexity.

To create a mind map for your writing project, follow these steps:

Step 1: Begin with a central idea or theme in the centre of the page Identify the core concept or theme around which your story or article revolves. Write this idea in the centre of a blank page or digital canvas, leaving ample space around it for additional layers of ideas and connections.

Step 2: Draw branches outward to represent related concepts or subtopics From the central idea, create branches that extend outward to represent related concepts or subtopics. These could include character relationships, plot points, thematic elements, or specific arguments and evidence in non-fiction writing.

Step 3: Add additional layers of branches to explore further details or con-

nections As you delve deeper into each subtopic, add further layers of branches to represent more specific details or connections. This hierarchical structure allows you to visualize the relationships between various elements within your work, fostering a greater understanding of how each component contributes to the overall narrative or argument.

Step 4: Use colours, images, or symbols to enhance your map and reinforce connections To make your mind map more visually engaging and memorable, incorporate colours, images, or symbols that represent specific ideas, characters, or themes. These visual elements can help you quickly identify connections and patterns within your work, streamlining the planning process and stimulating creative thinking.

By embracing mind mapping as a planning tool, you can approach your writing project with a fresh perspective and a greater sense of organization. This visual method enables you to explore the intricate web of connections within your story or article, promoting innovative thinking and fostering a deeper understanding of your work's structure and content. Whether used in conjunction with other planning techniques or as a standalone method, mind mapping can be a powerful tool in your writing arsenal, helping you to craft compelling stories and transform your writing skills.

The Snowflake Method

The snowflake method offers a unique and iterative approach to planning that can help you gradually build your story or article from a single, central idea. This method is particularly effective for writers who prefer to develop their work incrementally, allowing them to add complexity and depth to their narrative or argument with each step.

To use the snowflake method in your writing project, follow these steps:

Step 1: Begin with a one-sentence summary of your story or article Craft a concise, yet informative sentence that encapsulates the essence of your narrative or argument. This summary will serve as the foundation for your plan, providing a clear and focused starting point from which to build.

Step 2: Expand the summary into a full paragraph, including key plot points or ideas Elaborate on your initial summary by developing a full paragraph that outlines the main plot points, character arcs, or central ideas of your work. This expanded summary will help you identify the critical components of your narrative or argument, paving the way for further development.

Step 3: Develop a one-page outline for each of the main characters or sections For fiction writing, create a one-page outline for each of the primary characters, detailing their backgrounds, motivations, and roles within the story. For non-fiction writing, prepare a one-page outline for each of the main sections or arguments, highlighting the supporting evidence and key takeaways.

Step 4: Write a detailed synopsis, incorporating the character outlines and plot developments With your character or section outlines in place, draft a comprehensive synopsis that weaves together the various elements of your story or article. This synopsis should provide a clear and coherent overview of your work, ensuring that all critical components are effectively integrated.

Step 5: Continue expanding and refining your plan until you have a comprehensive roadmap for your writing As you work through the snowflake method, your plan will become increasingly detailed and complex. Continue expanding and refining your plan until you have a thorough and well-organized roadmap that guides you through the writing process, ensuring that all aspects of your story or article are fully developed and coherent.

By embracing the snowflake method, you can approach your writing project with a sense of structure and direction, gradually building your narrative or argument from a single, central idea. This iterative planning process allows you to explore the intricacies of your story or article in a systematic and organized manner, providing a solid foundation upon which to craft your final work. As you incorporate the snowflake method into your writing routine, you'll be well on your way to crafting compelling stories and transforming your writing skills.

The Free Writing or Pantsing Method

The free writing or "pantsing" (writing by the seat of your pants) method is an alternative approach that encourages spontaneity and creative exploration. This method is particularly appealing to writers who prefer to discover their story or argument as they write, allowing their ideas to evolve and develop organically.

To employ the free writing or pantsing method in your writing project, consider the following suggestions:

Step 1: Begin with a general idea or theme Instead of starting with a detailed outline or synopsis, initiate your writing process with a broad concept, theme, or character. This will provide a loose framework for your story or article, granting you the freedom to explore various narrative paths and ideas as they emerge.

Step 2: Write without inhibition Embrace the spontaneity of free writing by allowing your thoughts to flow freely onto the page or screen. Avoid self-editing or second-guessing your ideas as you write, focusing instead on capturing the essence of your story or argument as it unfolds in your mind.

Step 3: Trust your instincts As you navigate the twists and turns of your narrative or argument, trust your instincts to guide you in the right direction. The "pantsing" method relies heavily on intuition and creative exploration, so be open to following unexpected paths and discovering new connections as you write.

Step 4: Set aside dedicated writing time To maximize the benefits of free writing, commit to regular writing sessions during which you can immerse yourself in your story or article without interruption. These focused periods will enable you to maintain your creative momentum and more effectively develop your ideas.

Step 5: Revisit and revise your work
Although the "pantsing" method encourages spontaneity and creative freedom, it is still essential to review and revise your work after the initial drafting process. Once you have completed your first draft, take the time to read through your manuscript,

identifying any inconsistencies, gaps, or areas that require further development.

Step 6: Be open to restructuring As you review and revise your work, be prepared to make significant structural changes, such as rearranging sections, adding or removing characters, or altering the narrative's timeline. These adjustments will help you refine your story or article, ensuring that it is well-organized and compelling.

By embracing the free writing or pantsing method, you can embark on a writing journey that prioritizes creative exploration and discovery. This approach enables you to immerse yourself in the storytelling process, allowing your narrative or argument to develop and evolve naturally. While the pantsing method may require more extensive revision and restructuring than more structured planning techniques, it offers a unique and engaging writing experience that can help you craft compelling stories and transform your writing skills.

The Scene-by-Scene Method

The scene-by-scene method is another valuable planning technique that focuses on organizing your story or article into individual scenes or segments. This method allows writers to visualize and develop their work in a modular and manageable way, ensuring that each scene or section contributes effectively to the overall narrative or argument.

To implement the scene-by-scene method in your writing project, follow these steps:

Step 1: Break down your story or article into individual scenes or sections Begin by identifying the key scenes or sections that make up your narrative or argument. These can include pivotal plot points, character introductions, important revelations, or crucial transitions within your work.

Step 2: Write a brief summary for each scene or section For each identified scene or section, craft a concise summary that highlights its primary purpose, the characters involved, and the events or ideas that occur within it. These summaries will serve as a blueprint for your writing, ensuring that you have a clear and focused understanding of each scene's role within the larger narrative or argument.

Step 3: Arrange your scenes or sections in a logical order Once you have completed your scene or section summaries, arrange them in a logical and coherent order that supports your story's pacing or your article's flow. This may involve rearranging scenes, adjusting the timeline, or even adding or removing scenes as needed.

Step 4: Flesh out each scene or section With your scene or section summaries in place and organized, begin expanding upon each one by adding dialogue, descriptions, or additional details as necessary. This will help you fully develop each scene or section, ensuring that it effectively contributes to your work's overall structure and content.

Step 5: Revise and refine your scenes or sections As you complete each scene or section, take the time to review and revise your work. Look for areas that could benefit from further development or clarification, and ensure that each scene or section seamlessly transitions to the next.

Step 6: Assemble your completed scenes or sections Once you have fully developed and revised each scene or section, assemble them in the order you determined earlier. This will provide you with a complete draft of your story or article, ready for further editing and refinement.

By employing the scene-by-scene method, you can approach your writing project with a structured and organized plan that focuses on individual scenes or sections. This modular planning technique allows you to concentrate on one piece of your story or argument at a time, ensuring that each component is effectively developed and integrated within your work. As you incorporate the scene-by-scene method into your writing routine, you'll be well on your way to crafting compelling stories and transforming your writing skills.

Creating an Effective Writing Plan

An effective writing plan serves as the backbone of your writing project, helping you stay organized, focused, and motivated throughout the process. By following the guidelines below, you can create a writing plan that supports your unique approach and sets you on the path to success:

Rule 1: Be flexible and adaptable Regardless of the planning method you choose, remember that your writing plan should be fluid and adaptable. As your ideas evolve or new insights emerge, be open to revising and adjusting your plan accordingly. This will ensure that your writing remains dynamic, engaging, and true to your creative vision.

Rule 2: Clearly define your goals and objectives Before diving into the details of your writing plan, take the time to identify and articulate your primary goals and objectives. Are you aiming to complete a novel, write a series of articles, or explore a specific theme or concept? By clarifying your intentions from the outset, you can create a focused and purposeful writing plan that aligns with your aspirations.

Rule 3: Include a timeline or schedule To maintain momentum and stay on track, incorporate a timeline or schedule into your writing plan. Determine realistic deadlines for key milestones, such as completing an outline, finishing a first draft, or submitting your work for publication. By breaking your project down into manageable tasks with clear deadlines, you can maintain a steady pace and monitor your progress throughout the writing process.

Rule 4: Address potential challenges or obstacles As you develop your writing plan, consider any potential challenges or obstacles you may encounter along the way. These could include time constraints, writer's block, or gaps in your knowledge or understanding. By identifying these hurdles in advance, you can proactively develop strategies to overcome them and minimize their impact on your writing journey.

Rule 5: Incorporate routine and self-discipline Establish a writing routine that works for you, whether it involves setting aside specific times each day, writing in short bursts, or aiming for a certain word count per session. Consistency and self-discipline are key factors in maintaining your momentum and ensuring steady progress toward your goals.

Rule 6: Seek feedback and support Engage with writing communities, friends, or mentors to share your progress, discuss challenges, and seek constructive feedback on your work. This will not only provide valuable insights for improvement but also help you stay motivated and accountable.

By incorporating these elements into your writing plan, you will create a strong foundation that supports your writing project from start to finish. With a well-crafted plan in place, you'll be better equipped to navigate the twists and turns of the writing process, ultimately producing compelling stories and transforming your writing skills.

Mastering Through Research

In writing, as in medicine, we often think of creativity and technique as two separate entities. We assume that creativity is the realm of the artist, while technique belongs to the technician. But in truth, the best writing emerges from a balance of both creativity and technique. This is where research comes in. By conducting thorough research, we can infuse our writing with the depth and richness that comes from real-world experience. We can ground our stories in reality, and use our imagination to elevate them to something truly compelling. In this chapter, we'll explore the power of research in the writing process, and learn how to use it to craft stories that captivate and inspire.

The Importance of Research

Thorough research is a crucial component of the writing process, as it provides the foundation upon which compelling, authentic, and well-informed stories or articles are built. By investing time and effort into conducting comprehensive research, you can elevate your writing and ensure that your work resonates with readers. In this section, we will examine the various reasons why research is essential to the success of your writing project.

Enhance credibility and accuracy Well-researched writing is more likely to be perceived as credible and trustworthy by readers. By gathering accurate information and supporting your ideas with reliable sources, you demonstrate a commitment to accuracy and intellectual integrity, which in turn fosters reader trust and confidence in your work.

Strengthen your arguments and ideas Research equips you with the necessary evidence and examples to substantiate your arguments, claims, or ideas. By presenting well-supported and data-driven points, you can make a stronger, more persuasive case to your readers, ensuring that your message is both compelling and convincing.

Foster depth and complexity Thorough research allows you to explore your topic or theme in greater depth, uncovering nuances, subtleties, and complexities that might otherwise be overlooked. This added layer of depth can make your writing richer, more engaging, and ultimately more satisfying for your readers.

Illuminate new perspectives and insights As you delve into your research, you may encounter alternative viewpoints, fresh ideas, or innovative approaches that can enhance or even transform your original concept. By incorporating these new perspectives into your writing, you can create a more multifaceted, thought-provoking, and dynamic work.

Bolster your confidence as a writer A solid foundation of research can provide you with the confidence and assurance you need to tackle your writing project head-on. Armed with a wealth of information, you can approach your topic with authority and expertise, knowing that you have the knowledge and resources to back up your claims and ideas.

Avoid potential pitfalls Research can also help you identify potential pitfalls, inaccuracies, or misconceptions within your writing. By addressing these issues during the research phase, you can preemptively correct them, ensuring that your final work is polished, error-free, and well-informed.

Thorough research is an indispensable aspect of the writing process that can significantly impact the quality, credibility, and effectiveness of your work. By recognizing and embracing the importance of research, you will be better equipped to craft compelling, insightful, and well-informed stories or articles that engage and captivate your readers. As you continue on your writing journey, never underestimate the power of research to transform and elevate your work.

Conducting Effective Research

Conducting effective research is an essential skill that can greatly enhance the quality and credibility of your writing. To ensure that your research is thorough, accurate, and well-organized, follow these steps:

Step 1: Identify your research question or objective Begin by clarifying the primary question or objective you wish to address in your writing. This will help you focus your research efforts and ensure that you gather the most relevant and valuable information.

Step 2: Gather background information from reputable sources Start by obtaining a broad understanding of your topic or theme from reputable sources such as books, academic journals, and expert-authored websites. This initial research will help you familiarize yourself with the subject, identify key terms and concepts, and provide a solid foundation for more in-depth exploration.

Step 3: Use a variety of sources To gain a comprehensive and nuanced understanding of your topic, consult a diverse range of sources, including books, articles, websites, interviews, and primary documents. By drawing on multiple perspectives and types of information, you can ensure that your research is well-rounded, balanced, and accurate.

Step 4: Take detailed notes and keep track of your sources for citation purposes As you conduct your research, take detailed notes on the information you gather, making sure to document the source of each piece of information. This will make it easier to cite your sources accurately and avoid plagiarism when you incorporate the research into your writing. Additionally, taking notes helps you process and retain the information, making it more accessible when you need it.

Step 5: Stay organized by using tools like citation managers, spreadsheets, or note-taking apps Organizing your research is crucial to ensuring that you can quickly and easily locate the information you require as you write. Use tools such as citation managers (e.g., Zotero, Mendeley), spreadsheets, or note-taking apps (e.g., Evernote, Obsidian) to categorize, store, and manage your research materials. These tools can help you streamline your research process, prevent information overload, and maintain a clear and organized workspace.

Step 6: Evaluate your sources critically Not all sources are created equal, so it's essential to evaluate the credibility, reliability, and relevance of each source you consult. Consider factors such as the author's expertise, the publication date, and the overall quality of the source. Be wary of biased or outdated information, and strive to use only the most accurate and trustworthy sources in your research.

Step 7: Synthesize and analyse your findings As you gather information, take the time to synthesize and analyse your findings, looking for patterns, connections, and insights that can inform your writing. This process will help you identify the most important points to include in your work, as well as any gaps in your understanding that may require further research.

By following these steps and honing your research skills, you will be well-equipped to conduct thorough, effective research that provides a solid foundation for your writing. With a wealth of accurate, relevant, and well-organized information at your fingertips, you can craft compelling, well-informed stories that captivate and engage your readers.

Evaluating Sources

The quality and reliability of the sources you use in your research will directly impact the credibility of your writing. To ensure that you are using the most accurate, trustworthy, and relevant sources, it's essential to evaluate each source carefully. When assessing the value and reliability of a source, consider the following criteria:

Authority Investigate the author's credentials and expertise in the subject. Are they a recognized expert or scholar in the field? Do they have relevant education, professional experience, or a history of publications on the topic? A source written by a credible and knowledgeable author is more likely to be reliable and accurate.

Objectivity Consider the potential bias or impartiality of the source. Is the author presenting a balanced, objective view, or are they promoting a particular agenda or perspective? Be cautious of sources that display a strong bias or fail to consider alternative viewpoints, as these may not provide a comprehensive or accurate understanding of the topic.

Accuracy Assess the veracity of the facts and data presented in the source. Are the claims and assertions supported by evidence, such as citations, statistics, or examples? Can you independently verify the information through other reputable sources? Accurate and well-supported sources are essential for building a solid foundation for your writing.

Currency Evaluate the timeliness and relevance of the information in the source. Is the information up-to-date, or has it been superseded by more recent research or developments? For some topics, particularly those related to science, technology, or current events, using the most current information is vital for ensuring the accuracy and relevance of your research.

Relevance Finally, consider the extent to which the source contributes valuable information to your research. Does it address your research question or objective directly, or is it only tangentially related to your topic? Focus on sources that provide the most pertinent and insightful information, as these will have the greatest impact on the quality of your writing.

By applying these criteria when evaluating sources, you can ensure that you are using the most reliable, accurate, and relevant information in your research. This, in turn, will help you craft well-informed, credible, and compelling stories or articles that resonate with your readers and stand up to scrutiny. Remember that the quality of your research is directly linked to the quality of your writing, so invest the time and effort to evaluate your sources thoroughly and critically.

Integrating Research into Your Writing

Integrating research effectively into your writing is critical for creating compelling, well-informed stories and articles. By weaving your research findings seamlessly into your narrative, you can enhance the credibility, depth, and interest of your work. To successfully incorporate your research into your writing, consider the following tips:

Use evidence and examples to support your claims or arguments Your research findings should serve as the foundation for your claims, arguments, or observations. Use specific examples, statistics, or quotations from your research to support and substantiate your points. This will not only make your writing more persuasive and credible, but also help your readers understand and engage with the subject.

Cite your sources to provide credibility and avoid plagiarism When you include information, ideas, or quotes from your research in your writing, it's essential to give proper credit to the original source. Citing your sources not only lends credibility to your work but also helps you avoid plagiarism, a serious offense in the world of writing. Be sure to follow the appropriate citation style (e.g., APA, MLA, Chicago) as required by your specific project or publication.

Be mindful of your audience's prior knowledge and adjust your writing accordingly As you integrate research into your writing, consider your target audience's level of familiarity with the subject matter. If your readers are likely to be well-versed in the topic, you may need to provide less background information and focus on more advanced concepts or insights. Conversely, if your readers are new to the subject, ensure that you provide enough context and explanation to make your writing accessible and engaging.

Maintain a balance between your own voice and the information you present from your research While it's essential to include research findings in your work, remember that your writing should still reflect your unique perspective and voice. Be careful not to let your research overshadow your own thoughts and ideas. Strive to strike a balance between presenting the information you've gathered and offering your own analysis, interpretation, or insights.

By keeping these tips in mind as you integrate research into your writing, you can create well-informed, credible, and engaging stories or articles that resonate with your readers. By skillfully incorporating your research findings into your narrative, you can provide valuable context, depth, and authority, elevating your writing to new heights of quality and impact.

Mastering thorough research is an indispensable skill for any writer looking to create compelling and impactful stories or articles. By understanding the importance of research, conducting effective research, evaluating sources carefully, and integrating your findings seamlessly into your writing, you can significantly enhance the credibility, depth, and interest of your work. As you continue to develop your research skills, you will find that your writing becomes more informed, persuasive, and engaging, enabling you to craft stories and articles that captivate your readers and leave a lasting impression.

Writing with Care: Techniques for Compelling Stories

Writing is a craft, and like any craft, it requires care and attention to detail. Every word, sentence, and paragraph should be carefully crafted to ensure that it serves a purpose and contributes to the overall impact of the story. In this chapter, we'll explore some of the techniques that can help us write with care and create stories that truly captivate our readers. We'll look at the power of language, the importance of pacing and structure, and the role of detail in bringing stories to life. By mastering these techniques, we can take our writing to the next level and create stories that resonate with our readers long after they've finished reading.

Crafting Engaging Narratives

Writing engaging narratives is at the heart of captivating your audience and making your stories memorable. By using various techniques, you can create a compelling narrative that resonates with your readers. Consider the following strategies to enhance the impact of your storytelling:

Use strong, active verbs to propel your story forward Active verbs bring energy and momentum to your writing, making your story feel alive and dynamic. By using strong, action-oriented language, you can convey a sense of immediacy and movement that keeps your reader engaged and eager to know what happens next.

Vary your sentence structure and length for rhythm and pacing Monotonous sentence structures can make your writing feel flat and dull. By varying the structure and length of your sentences, you can create a sense of rhythm and pacing that helps to maintain your reader's interest. Short, crisp sentences can heighten tension or urgency, while longer, more complex sentences can slow the pace and allow for more detailed descriptions or introspection.

Employ vivid descriptions and sensory details to immerse your reader in the

story By painting a vivid picture of your story's setting, characters, and events, you can transport your reader into the world you've created. Use sensory details to evoke sights, sounds, smells, tastes, and textures, and don't shy away from using figurative language or unique imagery to make your descriptions more evocative and memorable.

Create relatable, well-developed characters with unique voices and motivations Your characters are the heart of your story, and well-developed, relatable characters can make your narrative come alive. Invest time in fleshing out your characters' backgrounds, desires, fears, and quirks. Give them unique voices that reflect their personalities, and ensure that their actions and motivations are believable and consistent.

Build tension and conflict to keep your reader invested in the outcome Tension and conflict are the driving forces behind any compelling narrative. By creating obstacles, challenges, or dilemmas for your characters, you can keep your readers emotionally invested in your story and eager to see how it unfolds. Don't be afraid to raise the stakes or introduce unexpected twists and turns to maintain a sense of suspense and intrigue.

By employing these techniques, you can craft engaging narratives that capture your reader's imagination and create a lasting impact. Remember, the key to great storytelling lies in your ability to weave together compelling characters, vivid descriptions, and a well-paced plot that keeps your audience invested in the story from beginning to end.

The Power of Storytelling

Storytelling is an age-old tradition that has captivated humans for centuries. It has the unique ability to connect people, evoke emotions, and inspire change. Understanding the power of storytelling and harnessing it in your writing can elevate your work to new heights, ensuring your stories resonate with readers and leave a lasting impact. In this section, we will explore the various elements that contribute to powerful storytelling, discuss the importance of narrative structure, and examine how to create stories that not only entertain but also enlighten and inspire. By honing your storytelling skills, you can craft compelling narratives that grip your audience and linger in their minds long after the final page has been turned.

Understand the classic storytelling structure, including exposition, rising action, climax, falling action, and resolution Familiarize yourself with the classic narrative arc, which serves as the backbone for many powerful stories. In the exposition, you introduce the characters, setting, and the central conflict. The rising action sees the development of tension, as the characters face obstacles and complications. The climax is the turning point or the moment of highest emotional intensity, often involving a significant confrontation or decision. The falling action consists of events that result from the climax, leading to the resolution, where the main conflicts are resolved, and the story concludes. By incorporating this structure, you can create a well-paced narrative that keeps your readers engaged.

Use anecdotes and personal experiences to illustrate your points Anecdotes and personal experiences can add depth, authenticity, and relatability to your writing. By sharing your own stories or those of others, you can make abstract concepts more tangible and provide compelling evidence to support your points. Anecdotes can also help to humanize your writing, allowing readers to see themselves in your stories and connect with your message on a personal level.

Tap into universal themes and emotions to create an emotional connection with your reader Powerful stories often revolve around universal themes and emotions, such as love, loss, fear, ambition, or redemption. By tapping into these shared experiences, you can forge an emotional connection with your readers, making your stories more meaningful and memorable. Consider exploring these themes through your characters, plot, or setting, and use emotional language to evoke empathy and emotional engagement from your readers.

By understanding the classic storytelling structure, utilizing anecdotes and personal experiences, and tapping into universal themes and emotions, you can harness the power of storytelling in your writing. This will allow you to craft compelling narratives that resonate with your readers, leaving a lasting impression and sparking meaningful connections. Remember, at the heart of every great story is the ability to elicit emotions, provoke thought, and inspire your audience to see the world through a different lens.

Revision: The Key to Polished Writing

The writing process doesn't end once you've completed your first draft; in fact, it's just the beginning. Revision is a crucial aspect of refining your work and transforming it from a rough sketch to a polished masterpiece. Through the process of revising, you will hone your narrative, clarify your message, and ensure that your writing is engaging and effective. In this section, we will discuss the importance of revision, offer strategies for approaching the revision process, and provide tips for identifying areas that need improvement. By embracing the art of revision, you will elevate your writing skills, craft more compelling stories, and ultimately produce a final product that stands the test of time.

Take a break between drafts to gain a fresh perspective After completing your initial draft, it's important to step away from your work for a while. This break allows you to distance yourself from your writing and return with a fresh perspective, making it easier to identify issues or areas for improvement. Whether it's a few hours or a few days, taking a break will help you approach your work with fresh eyes and a more objective mindset.

Read your work aloud to identify awkward phrasing or inconsistencies Reading your work aloud can help you spot awkward phrasing, unclear sentences, or inconsistencies in tone, pacing, or character voice. As you read, pay close attention to how the words sound and flow together, and make note of any areas that feel unnatural or difficult to understand. This practice can also reveal repetitive sentence structures or overused words, allowing you to make adjustments for variety and engagement.

Seek feedback from peers, mentors, or writing groups Soliciting feedback from others can provide valuable insights into the strengths and weaknesses of your work. Sharing your writing with peers, mentors, or writing groups can help you identify areas that may be unclear, confusing, or unconvincing to your readers. Be open to constructive criticism and use the feedback you receive to guide your revisions and improve your writing.

Be willing to cut, rearrange, or rewrite sections as needed for clarity and coherence Effective revision often involves making tough decisions about what stays and what goes in your writing. Be prepared to cut or condense sections that don't contribute to the overall narrative or message, and consider rearranging or rewriting passages to enhance clarity and coherence. Remember, the goal is to create a polished, engaging piece of writing that clearly communicates your ideas and resonates with your readers.

By incorporating these techniques into your revision process, you can effectively refine your writing and create a polished, compelling final product. Embracing revision as an integral part of the writing journey will not only help you produce better stories but also enable you to grow and develop as a skilled writer.

Proofread Like a Pro: Strategies for Flawless Writing

The Importance of Proofreading

Proofreading is an essential step in the writing process and plays a vital role in ensuring that your work is polished, error-free, and ready for publication. A meticulously proofread piece of writing not only demonstrates your professionalism and dedication to quality, but it also shows your attention to detail and respect for your readers. Errors in grammar, punctuation, spelling, and formatting can detract from your message, distract your readers, and ultimately undermine your credibility as a writer.

By proofreading your work thoroughly, you can catch and correct these errors before they reach your audience, allowing you to present a final product that accurately reflects your skills and expertise. Additionally, the proofreading process can help you identify and address any lingering inconsistencies or ambiguities in your writing, ensuring that your message is clear and easily understood by your readers. In short, proofreading is a crucial investment in the quality of your writing and an essential step towards crafting compelling, flawless stories that resonate with your audience.

Techniques for Effective Proofreading

Proofreading is a critical component of the writing process, and to ensure your work is error-free and polished, it's essential to adopt effective proofreading techniques. Consider these strategies to enhance your proofreading skills:

1. **Take a break before proofreading** After completing your writing, step away from it for a short period. This allows you to approach your work with fresh eyes and an objective perspective, making it easier to spot errors and inconsistencies.
2. **Read your work out loud** Reading your text aloud can help you identify awkward phrasing, missing words, or grammatical errors that you might overlook when reading

silently.

3. **Use a checklist:** Create a systematic checklist to review your work for grammar, punctuation, spelling, and formatting. This ensures you address every aspect of your writing and prevents you from overlooking any errors.

4. **Proofread in multiple passes**: Instead of trying to catch all errors in one go, proofread your work in multiple passes, focusing on different aspects with each pass. For example, you might check for spelling errors in one pass, punctuation in another, and formatting in a third.

5. **Change the font, size, or formatting**: Altering the appearance of your document can make errors stand out, as your brain is less likely to gloss over familiar text. Experiment with different fonts, sizes, or formatting styles to help you spot mistakes more easily.

By employing these techniques, you can significantly improve the quality of your proofreading efforts, ensuring that your final work is polished, professional, and free of errors.

Enlisting Help

While self-proofreading is a crucial part of the writing process, having another person review your work can provide invaluable insights and catch errors that you may have overlooked. This additional reviewer can be a friend, family member, colleague, or professional editor. Their fresh perspective can reveal inconsistencies or mistakes that might have escaped your notice.

When seeking external feedback, it's essential to be open to criticism and willing to make necessary changes. Keep in mind that constructive feedback is an opportunity for growth and improvement, not a personal attack. Engage in a dialogue with your reviewer, asking for clarification or discussing alternatives when needed. Remember that the ultimate goal is to create the best possible version of your work.

Additionally, consider joining a writing group or participating in online writing communities where you can share your work and receive feedback from other writers. These forums can offer valuable insights, suggestions, and encouragement, helping you grow as a writer and refine your craft.

By enlisting help from others and being receptive to their feedback, you can significantly improve the quality of your work, ensuring that it's polished, engaging, and free of errors. This collaborative approach will not only enhance your final product but also help you develop as a writer, honing your skills and expanding your understanding of the craft.

This chapter has equipped you with valuable insights and techniques to refine your work to its best possible version. We have delved into the importance of proofreading, effective proofreading techniques, and the benefits of enlisting help from others. By incorporating these strategies into your writing process, you demonstrate professionalism, attention to detail, and a commitment to your readers. As you continue your journey as a writer, never underestimate the power of diligent proofreading in enhancing the overall quality and impact of your work. Remember that the final polish is what sets your writing apart and leaves a lasting impression on your audience.

Sharing Your Work: How to Reach a Wide Audience

The Value of Sharing Your Work

Sharing your work is the final, yet crucial, step in the writing process. It's the moment when your words come to life and resonate with readers, creating a connection that transcends the pages. By sharing your stories, you can engage with readers, gather invaluable feedback, and build a dedicated following that will support your growth as a writer. In this chapter, we will discuss the importance of sharing your work, as well as various strategies to help you reach a wider audience and make a lasting impact in the literary world.

Taking the leap to share your work can be intimidating, but it is essential for numerous reasons. First, it allows you to test your ideas and receive input from others, which can help refine your writing and strengthen your storytelling. Additionally, sharing your work enables you to build a network of like-minded individuals who share your passion and can offer support, collaboration, and encouragement. Finally, by sharing your writing, you contribute to the global conversation, inspiring others and adding your unique voice to the tapestry of human experience.

In this chapter, we will explore the different avenues for sharing your work, from traditional publishing to self-publishing and digital platforms, and provide tips on how to effectively promote your writing and reach a wide audience.

Choosing the Right Platform

Selecting the ideal platform for sharing your writing is crucial for maximizing your work's impact and reaching your target audience. With an abundance of options available, such as blogs, websites, social media, and online publishing platforms, it's essential to carefully consider which one is best suited for your unique needs and goals. As you explore your options, keep the following factors in mind:

Your target audience Identifying your target readership is the first step in choosing the right platform. Understand their preferences, habits, and where they are most likely to engage with your writing. For instance, if you're targeting young adults, social media platforms like Instagram or TikTok may be more effective than a personal blog.

The format and style of your work Different platforms cater to various content formats and styles. For example, if you write poetry, Instagram's visual format and limited character count may suit your work better than a long-form blog. Alternatively, if you write serialized fiction, a platform like Wattpad might be more appropriate.

The potential reach and visibility of the platform Some platforms have wider reach and greater visibility than others, making it easier for readers to discover your work. Research each platform's user base and potential for organic growth to determine which one is likely to give your writing the most exposure.

As you weigh your options, remember that you can use multiple platforms to diversify your reach and connect with various reader segments. For example, you might maintain a blog for long-form content while utilizing social media for shorter pieces, updates, and reader engagement. By choosing the right platform(s) for your work, you can optimize your writing's impact and forge lasting connections with your audience.

Promoting Your Work

After selecting the most suitable platform for your work, it's crucial to promote it effectively to maximize visibility and draw in readers. Implement the following strategies to ensure your writing reaches a broader audience and creates an impact:

Step 1: Create a strong author bio and online presence Your author bio is often the first impression readers have of you. Craft a compelling and professional bio that highlights your expertise, interests, and writing style. Additionally, establish a consistent online presence across your chosen platform(s) and social media, showcasing your unique voice and engaging with your audience.

Step 2: Utilize social media platforms to share your work and engage with readers Share your writing on social media platforms like Twitter, Facebook, Instagram, and LinkedIn. Engage with readers by responding to comments, asking questions, and sharing insights into your writing process. This not only promotes your work, but also fosters a community of loyal readers.

Step 3: Network with other writers, influencers, and industry professionals Connect with fellow writers, influencers, and professionals within the writing and publishing industry. Attend conferences, workshops, and events to expand your network and learn from others. Collaborate with others on projects, interviews, or guest post on relevant websites to expand your reach and tap into new audiences.

Step 4: Participate in writing communities, forums, and groups Join online and offline writing communities, forums, and groups to connect with like-minded individuals, share your work, and gain valuable feedback. These communities can offer support, inspiration, and opportunities for cross-promotion, helping you reach new readers.

Content Marketing Develop valuable, informative, and engaging content related to your niche or genre to attract readers and establish yourself as an authority in your field. This could include blog posts, articles, videos, podcasts, or infographics. By consistently providing high-quality content, you can organically draw in readers who are interested in your subject matter. Over time, this will build trust and loyalty among your audience, encouraging them to explore and share your writing.

By employing these promotional strategies, you can ensure your writing reaches as many people as possible, allowing you to build a dedicated readership and elevate your writing career.

Engaging with Your Audience

Building a relationship with your audience is key to long-term success as a writer. By connecting with your readers on a personal level, you can create a loyal following that will support your work and help spread the word about your writing. Here are some ways to engage with your audience:

Responding to comments and messages Make it a priority to reply to reader comments and messages on your website, blog, or social media platforms. This shows that you value their opinions and are willing to engage in conversation, which can lead to further discussions and insights.

Encouraging feedback and discussions Ask open-ended questions and invite readers to share their thoughts on your work. This can help generate valuable feedback and foster a sense of community around your writing.

Providing regular updates and new content to maintain interest Keep your readers engaged by consistently publishing new material and sharing updates about your writing process or upcoming projects. This helps to maintain their interest and ensures that they stay connected with your work.

Offering exclusive content or incentives for subscribers or followers Reward your most loyal readers by providing exclusive content, discounts, or other incentives. This could include behind-the-scenes looks at your writing process, early access to new work, or bonus material related to your stories.

Organizing events, workshops, or webinars to connect with your audience on a deeper level Host live events, such as workshops, webinars, or Q&A sessions, to share your expertise and connect with your readers in a more personal setting. This can help you build a stronger rapport with your audience and demonstrate your passion and commitment to your craft.

By actively engaging with your audience and fostering a sense of community, you can create a strong support system for your work and ensure that your writing continues to resonate with readers.

Sharing your work and reaching a wide audience is an essential aspect of the writing process. By selecting the right platform, effectively promoting your work, and engaging with your audience, you can create a loyal following and enhance your writing career. Remember, it's not just about putting words on paper; it's also about connecting with readers and providing them with stories that resonate. By applying the strategies outlined in this chapter, you can transform your writing skills and create compelling stories that captivate your audience and leave a lasting impact. Embrace the journey of sharing your work and watch as it transforms your writing and the lives of your readers.

Conclusion

This book has provided a comprehensive framework for creating engaging narratives that capture your audience's attention. By delving into the essential steps of planning, researching, writing with care, proofreading, and sharing your work, you have acquired valuable insights and techniques that will enable you to refine and elevate your writing abilities.

As you embark on your writing journey, it's important to recognize that growth comes from consistent practice, unwavering persistence, and an open mind, embracing both successes and failures as opportunities to learn and improve. By incorporating the techniques and strategies discussed in this book, you can effectively transform your writing skills, crafting captivating, polished stories that resonate deeply with your readers.

Remember that writing is a lifelong pursuit, and the process itself is as valuable as the final product. Stay curious, embrace the challenges, and never stop striving to write better stories. With dedication and persistence, you can unlock your full potential as a writer and make a lasting impact on the literary world.

Appendix

Further Reading

By exploring these resources, you can deepen your understanding of the writing process, learn new techniques, and continue to grow and develop as a writer.

Books

1. Bell, J. S. (2004). Plot & Structure: Techniques and exercises for crafting a plot that grips readers from start to finish. Writer's Digest Books.
2. Brookfield, S. (2012). Becoming a Critically Reflective Teacher. Jossey-Bass.
3. Goldberg, N. (2005). Writing Down the Bones: Freeing the Writer Within. Shambhala Publications.
4. King, S. (2000). On Writing: A Memoir of the Craft. Scribner.
5. Lamott, A. (1994). Bird by Bird: Some Instructions on Writing and Life. Anchor Books.
6. Rozakis, L. (1999). The Complete Idiot's Guide to Grammar and Style. Alpha Books.
7. Strunk, W., & White, E. B. (2000). The Elements of Style. Longman.
8. Zinsser, W. (2006). On Writing Well: The Classic Guide to Writing Nonfiction. Harper Perennial.

Online Sites

1. Writers' Digest (https://www.writersdigest.com)
2. The Write Practice (https://thewritepractice.com)
3. The Creative Penn (https://www.thecreativepenn.com)
4. Helping Writers Become Authors (https://www.helpingwritersbecomeauthors.com)
5. Jane Friedman (https://www.janefriedman.com)
6. Well-Storied (https://www.well-storied.com)
7. Writing Excuses (https://writingexcuses.com) - A podcast on writing techniques and advice.

Online writing courses

1. Coursera (https://www.coursera.org)
2. MasterClass (https://www.masterclass.com)
3. Skillshare (https://www.skillshare.com)
4. Udemy (https://www.udemy.com)
5. edX (https://www.edx.org)

Writing Exercises

Exercises you can perform on a routine basis to develop and grow as a skilful writer. By incorporating these exercises into your routine, you can develop and grow as a writer, honing your skills and expanding your creative repertoire. Remember to be patient with yourself and to practice consistently to see improvement over time.

1. **Freewriting:** Set a timer for 10-15 minutes and write continuously without stopping or editing yourself. This exercise helps you develop a writing habit, overcome writer's block, and generate new ideas.
2. **Daily Journaling:** Write a journal entry every day, reflecting on your thoughts, feelings, experiences, or observations. This practice can improve your writing fluency and help you develop a regular writing routine.
3. **Writing Prompts:** Use writing prompts to inspire new stories or ideas. There are many websites and books that provide prompts for various genres and topics. Write a short story, scene, or essay based on a prompt each day or week.
4. **Character Sketches:** Create detailed profiles for characters from your stories, including their appearance, background, motivations, and relationships. This exercise helps you develop well-rounded, believable characters.
5. **Scene Writing:** Choose a setting or situation and write a scene that takes place within it. Focus on using descriptive language, engaging dialogue, and strong pacing to bring the scene to life.
6. **Imitation:** Choose a passage from a favorite book or author and try to imitate their writing style. This exercise can help you identify and learn from the techniques of successful writers.
7. **Word Limit Challenge:** Write a complete story, scene, or essay within a spe-

cific word limit (e.g., 100 words, 500 words, or 1,000 words). This exercise encourages brevity and clarity in your writing.

8. **Revising and Editing**: Take a piece of your own writing and revise it, focusing on improving the structure, clarity, and style. Then, edit it for grammar, punctuation, and spelling. This exercise helps you develop your self-editing skills and understand the importance of the revision process.

9. **Sensory Details**: Write a short scene or description focusing on one specific sense (sight, sound, touch, taste, or smell). This exercise can help you practice incorporating sensory details into your writing, making it more vivid and immersive.

10. **Perspective Shift**: Choose a story or scene you've written and rewrite it from a different point of view or perspective. This could involve changing the narrative voice (e.g., first person to third person) or shifting the focus to another character. This exercise can help you explore different narrative techniques and enhance your understanding of character motivation.

11. **Dialogue Practice**: Write a conversation between two or more characters, focusing on making the dialogue engaging, realistic, and revealing of each character's personality. This exercise can help you improve your dialogue-writing skills.

12. **Flash Fiction**: Write very short stories (usually between 100 and 1,000 words) that have a clear beginning, middle, and end. This exercise helps you practice concise storytelling and forces you to focus on the most essential elements of a story.

13. **Story Expansion**: Take a short story or scene you've written and expand it into a longer piece, adding details, characters, subplots, or backstory. This exercise helps you develop your ability to create more complex narratives.

Tools

Essential tools that a person may need when they consider becoming a writer. By equipping yourself with these essential tools, you can create a solid foundation for your writing journey and set yourself up for success as you develop your craft and build your writing career.

1 **Writing software**: A good word processor or writing application is essential for any writer. Options range from basic word processing programs like Microsoft Word or Google Docs to specialized writing applications like Scrivener, Ulysses, or Final

Draft, which offer advanced features tailored to specific writing tasks.

2 **Grammar and spell-checking tools**: Tools like Grammarly, ProWritingAid, or Hemingway Editor can help you identify and correct grammar, spelling, and punctuation errors, as well as improve your overall writing style.

3 **Notebook and pen or digital note-taking app**: For jotting down ideas, observations, or outlines, a physical notebook and pen or a digital note-taking app like Evernote, OneNote, or Google Keep can be invaluable.

4 **A reliable computer or laptop**: Invest in a reliable computer or laptop with a comfortable keyboard and sufficient storage space for your writing projects.

5 **A comfortable workspace**: A designated, comfortable workspace with proper lighting, an ergonomic chair, and a clutter-free environment can help you stay focused and productive.

6 **Style guides and writing resources**: Style guides like The Chicago Manual of Style, The Elements of Style by Strunk & White, or the AP Stylebook can be useful resources for learning proper writing conventions and style. Other writing books, like On Writing by Stephen King or Bird by Bird by Anne Lamott, can provide inspiration and guidance.

7 **A planner or calendar**: Keeping track of deadlines, writing goals, and submissions can be made easier with a physical planner or a digital calendar like Google Calendar or Trello.

8 **Citation management software**: For academic or research-based writing, citation management software like Zotero, Mendeley, or EndNote can help you organize your sources, generate citations, and create bibliographies.

9 **Cloud storage or backup system**: To prevent the loss of your work, use cloud storage services like Google Drive, Dropbox, or iCloud, or regularly back up your files to an external hard drive or a USB flash drive.

10 **Writing community and feedback**: Joining writing groups, forums, or attending workshops can help you connect with other writers, receive feedback on your work, and stay motivated. Some popular online writing communities include Scribophile, Absolute Write, and the Writers' Cafe on Kboards.

11 **Time management tools**: Use time management tools like the Pomodoro Technique or apps like Focus@Will or Forest to help you stay focused and maintain productivity during your writing sessions.

12 **Reading materials**: Reading widely in your chosen genre or field can help you learn from successful writers, expand your vocabulary, and stay inspired. Keep a collection of books, articles, or essays to refer to for ideas and guidance.

13 **A dedicated email address**: Set up a professional email address specifically for

your writing-related correspondence, such as submissions, queries, or networking.
14 **A website or online portfolio**: Creating a website or online portfolio can help showcase your work, establish your online presence, and connect with readers, agents, or editors.

Online Services

There are numerous online platforms where authors can find services for their projects, ranging from editing and proofreading to cover design and marketing. By exploring these online watering holes, authors can find the services they need to help bring. Some popular communities include:

1 **Reedsy** (https://reedsy.com): Reedsy is a marketplace that connects authors with editors, designers, marketers, and other professionals in the publishing industry.
2 **Fiverr** (https://www.fiverr.com): Fiverr is a freelance platform where authors can find various services, including cover design, editing, marketing, and ghostwriting.
3 **Upwork** (https://www.upwork.com): Upwork is another freelance platform that connects authors with professionals offering services such as editing, proofreading, design, and marketing.
4 **99designs** (https://99designs.com): 99designs is a design marketplace where authors can find professional designers for their book covers and other design-related projects.
5 **Freelancer** (https://www.freelancer.com): Freelancer is a platform that connects authors with freelancers offering various services, including editing, cover design, and marketing.
6 **The Creative Penn** (https://www.thecreativepenn.com): Joanna Penn's website offers resources for authors, including recommendations for editors, designers, and other service providers.
7 **Writer's Digest** (https://www.writersdigest.com): Writer's Digest provides resources and services for authors, including writing courses, editorial services, and contests.
8 **Alliance of Independent Authors** (https://www.allianceindependentauthors.org): ALLi is a professional organization for self-publishing authors that offers resources, services, and a supportive community. They provide a directory of vetted service

providers, including editors, designers, and marketers.

9 **9. Kboards Writers' Café** (https://www.kboards.com): Kboards is a popular forum for authors, and the Writers' Café section often includes discussions and recommendations for service providers, as well as author collaborations and networking opportunities.

10 **Goodreads** (https://www.goodreads.com): Goodreads is a book-centric social networking site where authors can connect with readers and other authors. The site features various groups and forums where authors can discuss and recommend service providers.

11 **Facebook Groups** There are numerous Facebook groups dedicated to writing, self-publishing, and marketing, where authors can connect with professionals, share resources, and ask for recommendations.

12 **LinkedIn** (https://www.linkedin.com): LinkedIn is a professional networking platform where authors can search for and connect with service providers in the publishing industry.

13 **Twitter** (https://www.twitter.com): Twitter is a useful platform for authors to connect with other writers, service providers, and industry professionals. By following relevant hashtags and engaging in writing communities, authors can discover recommended services and providers.

14 **Author service review websites** Websites like The Independent Publishing Magazine (http://www.theindependentpublishingmagazine.com) and The Book Designer (https://www.thebookdesigner.com) provide reviews and recommendations for author services, including editing, design, and marketing.

For more information, please visit:

https://www.wordtangles.com

The Author Biswajit D Baruah

> The scariest moment is always just before you start. After that, things can only get better.
>
> —Stephen King

Biswajit Baruah is a writer based in Muscaat, Oman. With a passion for storytelling and a love of language, Biswajit has been writing, with a focus on helping aspiring writers unlock their full potential.

In addition to writing, Biswajit is an avid reader, a lover of travel, and an ultra-marathoner. When he isn't writing , he can often be found exploring local bookstore or hiking in the nearby mountains.

The 5-Step Writing Master Plan is Biswajit's first book, and he is excited to share his knowledge and experience with aspiring writers around the world.

An Important Final Note

Thank you for taking the time to read my book, *The 5-Step Writing Master Plan: Craft Compelling Stories and Transform Your Writing Skills.* I hope that it has been a valuable resource in your writing journey, and that it has inspired you to unleash your creativity and share your unique voice with the world.

If you have a moment, I would greatly appreciate it if you could share your thoughts on the book. Your feedback is incredibly valuable to me, as it helps me understand what worked well and what can be improved in future editions.

Specifically, I would love to hear your thoughts on the following questions:

What did you like about the book? Which sections or chapters resonated with you? **What can be improved?** Are there any areas where the book could be more clear, concise, or helpful? **To whom would you recommend the book?** Do you think it would be helpful for other aspiring writers, or for people in a specific genre or writing style?

Your feedback will not only help me improve future editions of the book, but will also help other writers who are considering whether this book is right for them. If you'd like to share your thoughts, please feel free to leave a review on the book's Amazon page or Goodreads, or send me an email directly.

Thank you again for your support, and I look forward to hearing your thoughts.

"Writing is an exploration. You start from nothing and learn as you go.

—E.L. Doctorow